COLORING BOOK FOR KID

Adventures
ARE FOR
Everyone

You don't have to be PERFECT
— to be —
AMAZING

It doesn't matter what others ARE DOING. It matters what you are DOING.

DON'T
QUIT

A QUITTER never WINS.
A WINNER never QUITS.

Girl
POWER!

YOU
CAN DO
AMAZING
THINGS

You are awesome

Stay
positive

Dance
LIKE NO ONE IS
watching

be-
you-
tiful

LEAVE
YOUR
fears
BEHIND

You are
STRONG

love

THERE IS
ALWAYS
HOPE

I can
AND
I will

BELIEVE
IN
YOURSELF

You are
BRAVE

SHE BELIEVED SHE COULD AND SO SHE DID

Be
COURAGEOUS

LOVE
YOURSELF

Make
YOUR OWN
magic

Be true
TO WHO
you are

Believe
YOU CAN
and you are
HALFWAY
there

SELF
LOVE
IS YOUR
SUPER
POWER

Life
is
tough,
but so are
YOU

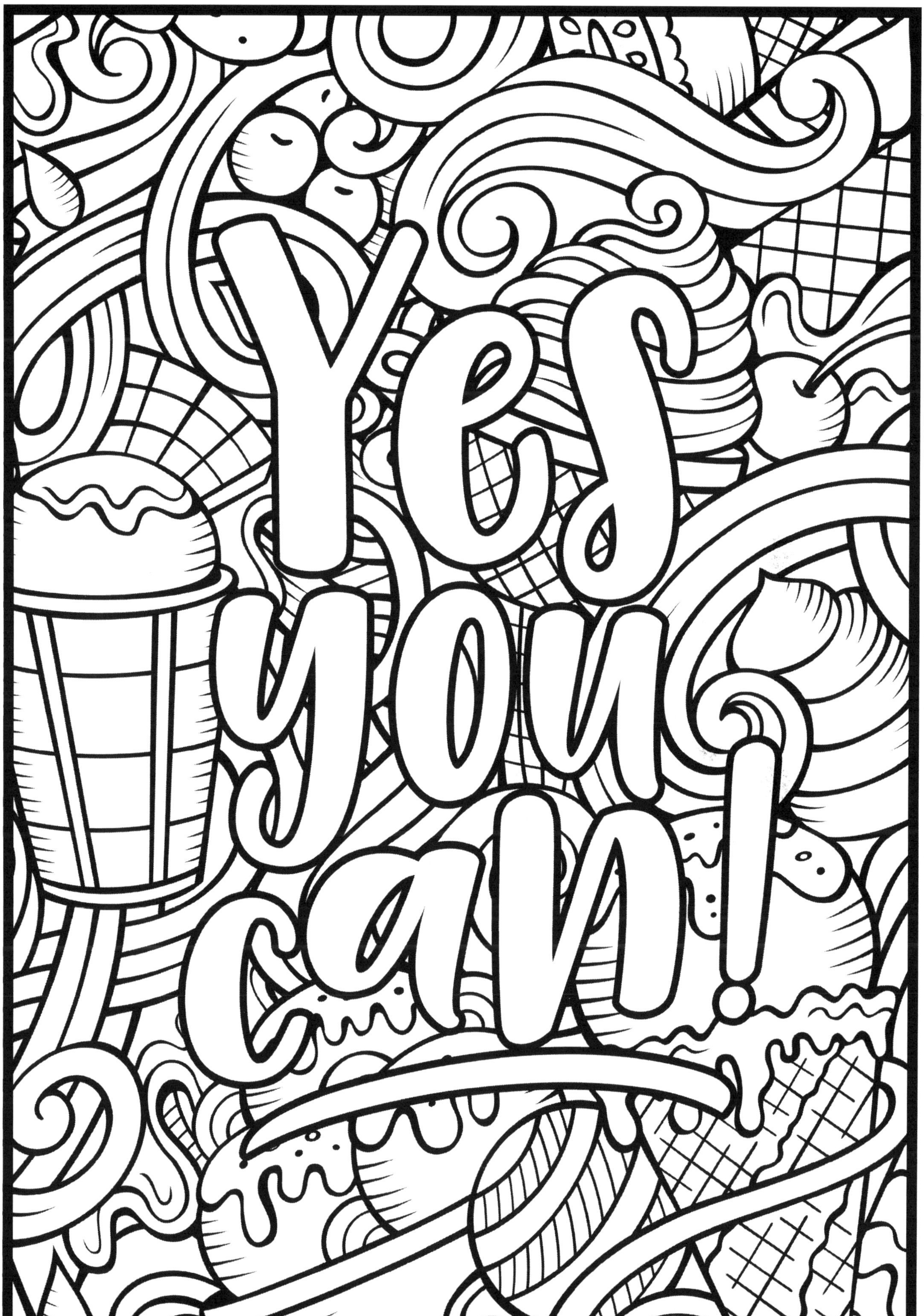
Yes you can!

You are
BEAUTIFUL

The best
view
comes
after the
hardest
CLIMB

AIM
HIGH
SHOOT
FOR THE
STARS

THERE'S IS
ALWAYS
something to be
THANKFUL
FOR

You got this

DREAM
big
WORK
hard

Mistakes
ARE PROOF THAT
YOU ARE
trying

YOU'RE
a limited
EDITION

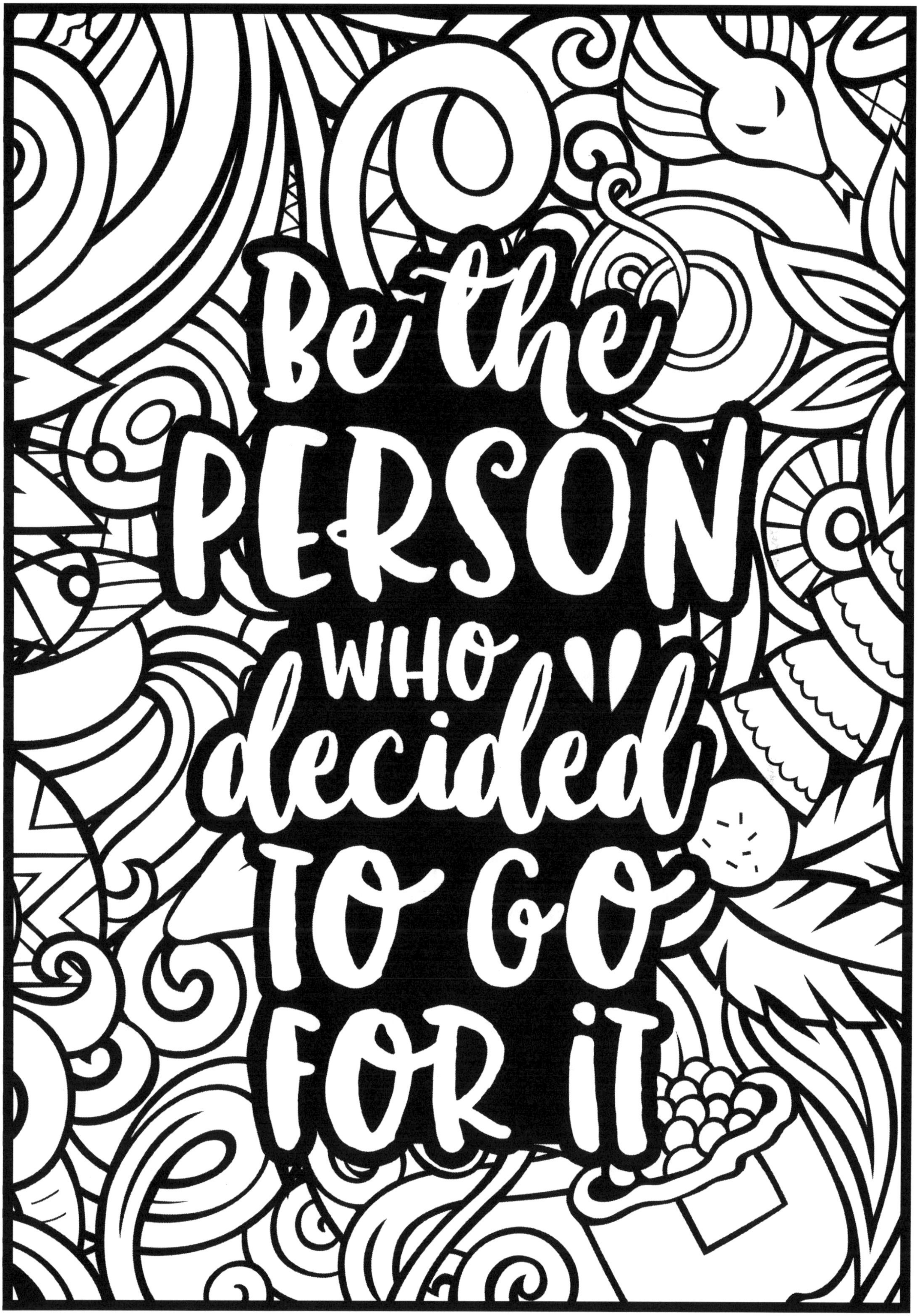
Be the
PERSON
WHO
decided
TO GO
FOR it

JUST
believe
IN YOURSELF

Have
COURAGE
and be
KIND